JOURNEY THROUGH *the*
ARK ENCOUNTER

Master Books®
A Division of New Leaf Publishing Group

Table of Contents

SPECIAL ACKNOWLEDGMENT:

We would like to offer special thanks to Tim Chaffey, Mike Belknap, and Stephanie McDorman of Answers in Genesis, for providing us with the text for this book.

First printing: June 2017
Third printing: November 2017

Copyright © 2017 by Answers in Genesis–USA. All rights reserved. No part of this book may be used or reproduced in any manner whatsoever without written permission of the publisher, except in the case of brief quotations in articles and reviews. For information write:
Master Books®, P.O. Box 726, Green Forest, AR 72638
Master Books® is a division of the New Leaf Publishing Group, Inc.

ISBN: 978-1-68344-012-3
ISBN: 978-1-61458-603-6 (digital)
Library of Congress Number: 2017906609
Cover & Interior by Left Coast Design

Unless otherwise noted, Scripture quotations are from the New King James Version of the Bible.
Please consider requesting that a copy of this volume be purchased by your local library system.

Printed in the United States of America

Please visit our website for other great titles:
www.masterbooks.com

For information regarding author interviews,
please contact the publicity department at (870) 438-5288.

Master Books®
A Division of New Leaf Publishing Group
www.masterbooks.com

PHOTO CREDITS:

Paul DeCesare & Maria Murphy

DECK FLOOR PLANS

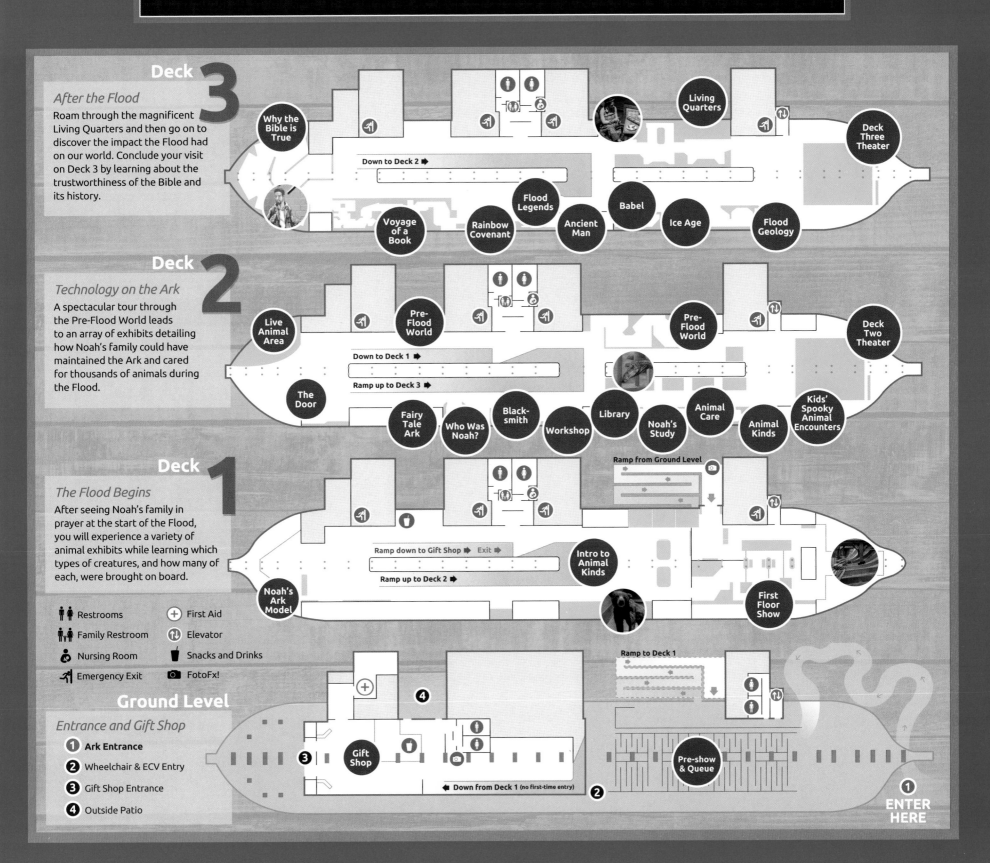

Deck 3

After the Flood

Roam through the magnificent Living Quarters and then go on to discover the impact the Flood had on our world. Conclude your visit on Deck 3 by learning about the trustworthiness of the Bible and its history.

Down to Deck 2 ➡

- Why the Bible is True
- Voyage of a Book
- Rainbow Covenant
- Flood Legends
- Ancient Man
- Babel
- Ice Age
- Flood Geology
- Living Quarters
- Deck Three Theater

Deck 2

Technology on the Ark

A spectacular tour through the Pre-Flood World leads to an array of exhibits detailing how Noah's family could have maintained the Ark and cared for thousands of animals during the Flood.

Down to Deck 1 ➡
Ramp up to Deck 3 ➡

- Live Animal Area
- The Door
- Pre-Flood World
- Fairy Tale Ark
- Who Was Noah?
- Black-smith
- Workshop
- Library
- Noah's Study
- Animal Care
- Pre-Flood World
- Animal Kinds
- Kids' Spooky Animal Encounters
- Deck Two Theater

Deck 1

The Flood Begins

After seeing Noah's family in prayer at the start of the Flood, you will experience a variety of animal exhibits while learning which types of creatures, and how many of each, were brought on board.

Ramp from Ground Level
Ramp down to Gift Shop   Exit ➡
Ramp up to Deck 2 ➡

- Noah's Ark Model
- Intro to Animal Kinds
- First Floor Show

Legend

- 👫 Restrooms
- 👪 Family Restroom
- 🤱 Nursing Room
- 🏃 Emergency Exit
- ➕ First Aid
- ↕ Elevator
- 🥤 Snacks and Drinks
- 📷 FotoFx!

Ground Level

Entrance and Gift Shop

1. Ark Entrance
2. Wheelchair & ECV Entry
3. Gift Shop Entrance
4. Outside Patio

- Gift Shop
- Ramp to Deck 1
- Pre-show & Queue
- ④ Outside Patio
- ③ Gift Shop Entrance

← Down from Deck 1 (no first-time entry)
② Wheelchair & ECV Entry

① ENTER HERE

Introduction

When I thought about the Ark Encounter and the design of the Ark and its interior, I tried to put myself in the place of Noah and imagine how he might have thought about the daunting responsibility that God had given him: to build a wooden ship that would house and feed the future of all humanity (he and his family) and the animal world that God would bring to him, a ship that would weather a global storm of monstrous proportions for an unknown period of time on the sea without means of a sail or rudder. What a man of faith and resources Noah must have been. The Bible says he was a man of faith, righteous in his generation, willing to surrender to God's call on his life and do as God commanded in a generation and culture that was totally antagonistic to God. He must have been mocked and ridiculed, yet for decades he faithfully worked to build the Ark with his family.

The walk through the Ark Encounter is the story of Noah and his family. Who was he and how did he accomplish this task? How was he trained for such a project? How did he know what to do? Did God give him a blueprint to follow or did God allow him to figure it out? How did he know how many animals would come, how much food to place on board, and what kind of food was required?

Each floor of the Ark tells a different part of Noah's journey. **Deck One** is filled with animal cages of various sizes, food stores in pots and bags, water storage, and everything needed to build a life over again: wagons, furniture, tools, raw materials, seeds, plants. The ship is full. God shuts the door, lightning flashes, thunder crashes, and the family prays for safety as the journey begins.

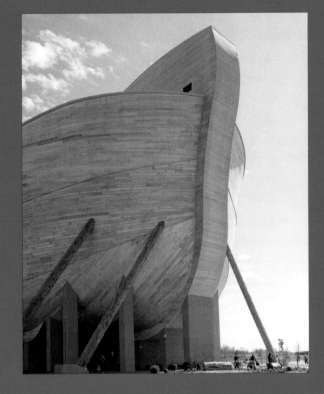

Deck Two focuses on how Noah could build the Ark and care for the animals during the Flood. How did he aquire the necessary skills to build the Ark? How did he provide clean air, sunlight, water distribution, and waste removal? How could eight people care for all the animals on the ship and themselves for over a year? The exhibits provide realistic and researched solutions.

Deck Three answers important questions related to the Flood and its effects on our world. Is there evidence for a global Flood? Was there an Ice Age? Was ancient man highly advanced? Most importantly, it explains the Gospel and the main purpose of the Ark Encounter: to lead people to Christ—our Ark who brings us through this life to eternal safety if we place our trust in Him.

We live in a world that is becoming more negative towards biblical truth each day, and my prayer is that your faith will be renewed as you walk through this one-of-a-kind display of biblical history. The Ark was real, Noah's Flood was real, and God's Word is real. May the God of all truth richly bless you this day.

Patrick Marsh

Vice President of Attractions Design for the Creation Museum and the Ark Encounter

⟫⟫ ARK EXTERIOR *and* GROUNDS ⟪⟪

Catching sight of this engineering marvel from the shuttle bus shatters childhood notions of a cute little bathtub ark. Stretching 510 feet in length, 85 feet in width, and 51 feet in height, this Ark was built to biblical proportions, literally.

On July 5, 2016, the board of directors of Answers in Genesis laid these 12 stones as a memorial to God's provision, recalling the Lord's instruction to the Israelites after they crossed the Jordan River. ▼

The bow end of the Ark, as seen from the back, provides visitors with a great view of the bow fin and the exterior made of radiata pine from New Zealand.

Reaching just over 100 feet high at the top of the bow fin, the Ark stands about as tall as a ten-story building. The view of this massive structure from the front of Emzara's Kitchen helps guests understand how Noah could have fit all those animals on board.

The ramp shows how Noah's family and the animals may have boarded the Ark. ▶

A beautiful view of the bow from behind the Ark. ▼

God instructed Noah to put a door in the side of the Ark. At the Ark Encounter, a representation of this door is found at the top of the ramp.

The location of the Ark Encounter among the hills of Kentucky affords some gorgeous photo opportunities that will only improve in time as more landscaping is completed around the structure.

The strategically placed viewing area in front of the lake allows guests to take in a spectacular view of the Ark and its reflection. This site is one of the most popular locations for family and large group photographs.

Stunning sunrises and sunsets are frequently witnessed at the property.

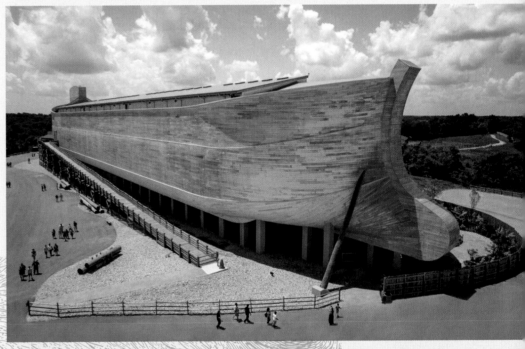

Queue and Ramp

Upon arriving at the Ark Encounter, guests enter the queue, which winds its way under the Ark and features a number of props that would have been helpful in building and loading the Ark. A large ramp leads to the first deck.

DECK ONE

Small Animal Cages

Meander through a maze of hundreds of small animal cages as the sounds of exotic creatures and a raging storm usher in a sense of awe and wonder.

Throughout the Ark, you will see devices that Noah and his family may have used for efficient animal care.

For these small cages, food and water could periodically be loaded into the boxes and clay jars, so the rations could be dispensed into containers in the cages as they were consumed.

First Floor Show

In contrast to the popular, overly cute Ark and Flood images the Ark Encounter immediately sets the somber, realistic tone of a family about to endure the greatest trial of their lives. See Noah gather his family for prayer when the rain started pounding outside the Ark.

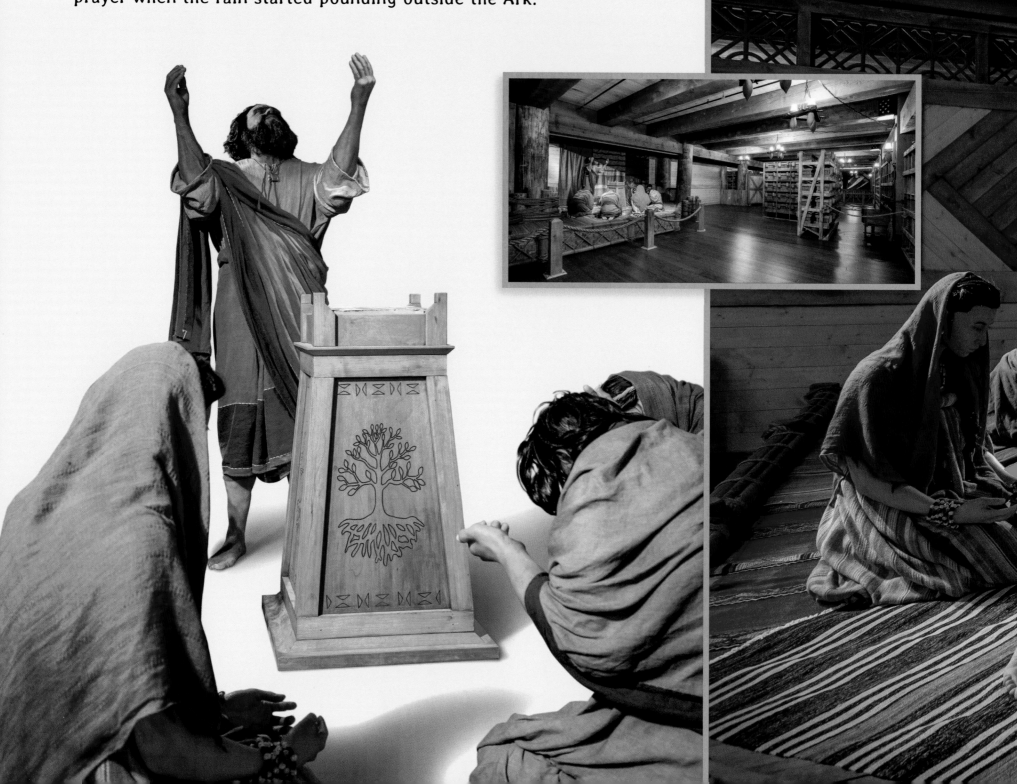

In this first encounter with Noah's family, you may notice the middle brown tone of their skin. Every person from all nations descended from the eight people on the Ark, so it makes sense to depict them with shades of middle brown skin, which would allow for a wide diversity of skin tones among their descendants.

Introduction to Animal Kinds

The large open area offers the first glimpses of the Ark's magnificent sculpted animals. Large cages line both sides of the hull. Cages on the port side contain familiar varieties, such as bears, sloths, deer, and pigs. The enclosures on the starboard side contain animals that have gone extinct since the Flood, such as pterosaurs and scutosaurs.

The cages feature signs with fun facts regarding their respective animal kinds. This area also contains large illustrated billboard signs to help guests understand which animals were required on the Ark, including the now-extinct animals mentioned above. But the marine creatures were not on board, and there was no need to bring large, full-grown adults of each kind.

Even the strange looking caseids, a family of non-mammalian synapsids, had a home on the Ark.

Every animal fabricated for the Ark Encounter is a carefully crafted reconstruction based on studies of the fossil remains.

Certain features of the Ark's animals may seem unusual, but most are all still recognizable as members of their respective kinds.

Some varieties of azhdarchid pterosaurs, like *Quetzalcoatlus northropi*, stood as tall as a giraffe and were the largest of all known flying creatures.

In addition to the large billboard signs, several smaller signs address common questions about the Ark. Visitors can learn how freshwater fish survived the Flood, whether insects were required on the Ark, if Noah brought 7 or 14 animals of each flying creature and clean animal, how Ark researchers determined the number of Ark animals, and much more.

The pig kind represented by *Platygonus*.

Storage

The Lord instructed Noah to take food for his family and for all the animals (Genesis 6:21). Much of the vessel would have been filled with foodstuffs, water, and other items.

The short, wide earthenware represent liquid storage containers. Oil from plants, such as olives, could have been stored as a fuel source for the lamps seen throughout the Ark. Most of the water could have been stored in cisterns on the second and third decks, but a backup supply of drinking water could have been held in these broad containers.

Throughout the Ark, stacks of storage bags like these represent the vast amount of seeds, nuts, and dried fruits and vegetables used as food for the people and animals.

Though there may be only one bat kind—order Chiroptera—the Ark Encounter more conservatively estimated them at the family rank, accounting for around two dozen kinds.

Bat Kinds

Determining the kind a particular animal belongs to can be a difficult task. Researchers used a worst-case approach that surely added greatly to the total number of animals. For example, although there may be just one bat kind, the bats were separated into about two dozen kinds, each represented by 14 animals.

Architecture in the Ark

The largest free-standing timber-frame structure in the world, the Ark consists of 3.1 million board feet of lumber. Laid end to end, this lumber would stretch from Williamstown, Kentucky to Philadelphia, Pennsylvania.

Hundreds of huge beams and logs support the structure. Some of the center "lodge poles," as seen here, are more than three feet in diameter and nearly 50 feet long!

The wooden "ribs" of the Ark seen in the picture below comprise the bottom of the "bents" that frame the Ark. Each half-bent weighs over 25,000 pounds and utilizes 1,200 pounds of bolts.

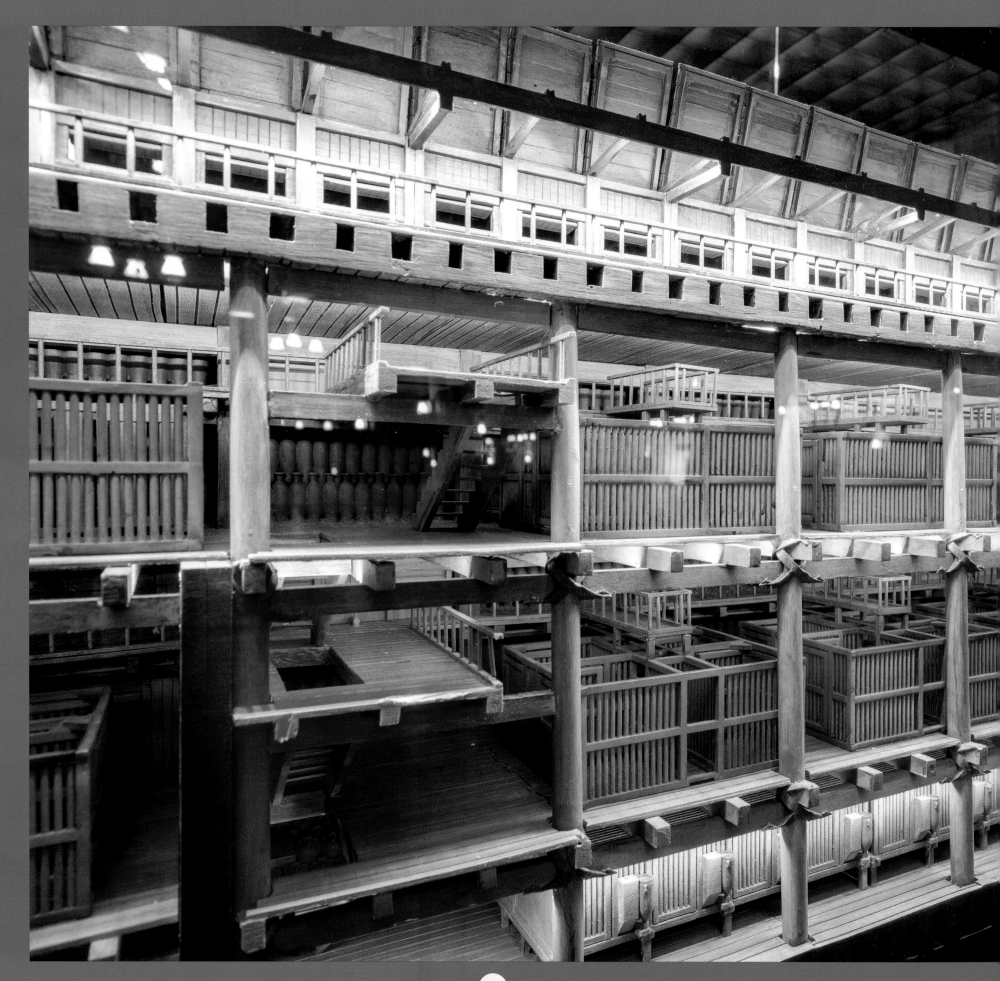

Noah's Ark Model

This large scale model displays how the real Ark may have been designed and organized. Many of the pieces were digitally sculpted and 3D-printed.

The model shows that the Ark had adequate space to meet the needs of the people and animals on board:

- ⚙ Living and working space for eight people

- ⚙ Enclosures to house nearly 7,000 animals and systems to care for them

- ⚙ Practical short ramps near bow and stern with steeper inclines between floors

- ⚙ Large cisterns to store and supply potable water

Pre-Flood World

This spectacular exhibit shows what the world may have looked like before the Flood. The Bible explains that God created everything in six days approximately 6,000 years ago, and initially, everything was "very good" (Genesis 1:31). There was no suffering, disease, bloodshed, or death. What went wrong?

DECK TWO

THE SERPENT SAID TO THE WOMAN, "YOU WILL NOT SURELY DIE."

GENESIS 3:4

Genesis 3 states that the serpent tempted the first woman to disobey God even though the penalty was death. The first man, Adam, joined her in rebelling against the Creator.

Adam's sin brought suffering, disease, bloodshed, and death into this world. Yet God demonstrated His mercy by covering them with a sacrifice. By clothing them with animal skins, God provided a vivid reminder of the cost of sin while foreshadowing how He would ultimately deal with sin and death.

As Adam and Eve's descendants multiplied, the world became an exceedingly wicked place. Genesis 4–6 details some of the evil activities prior to the Flood. The "Descent into Darkness" wall highlights six areas in which man corrupted his God-given abilities. For example, while music and metalworking are not inherently evil, they were likely used for immoral purposes in a sinful society.

Stunning artwork and magnificent dioramas featuring dozens of lifelike 3D-printed characters give visitors a glimpse into what the wicked pre-Flood world may have been like. This pagan temple diorama implies that the people may have engaged in child sacrifice and ritual prostitution.

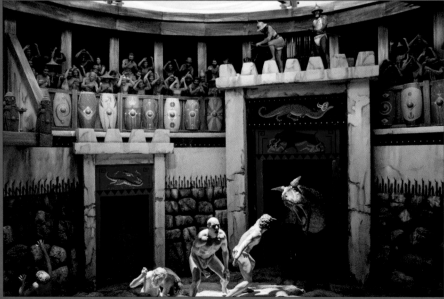

God said the world was filled with violence. This exhibit depicts a culture obsessed with death. In the arena diorama, a raucous crowd cheers on the awful fate of several people facing a terrifying end. Another diorama shows a society focused on living for pleasure rather than God.

Man's wickedness eventually brought God's judgment. He destroyed that world with the global Flood, but He also demonstrated His mercy by saving Noah's family and the animals aboard the Ark.

Kids' Spooky Animal Encounters

What might the Ark be like if some of the animals escaped from their enclosures while Noah's family slept? And not just any sort of animals—the creepiest animals. That's the theme of this fun exhibit for younger visitors.

The exhibit includes a creepy crawlspace, a cage for photo opportunities, some two-way mirrors for making goofy faces, and plenty of other surprises for the kids.

Here is a rare glimpse of what the exhibit looks like in the light. With the lights off, the windows seen here hold surprises for guests.

Pay close attention as you move through this exhibit to spot some unique critters, but prepare yourself for the unexpected. It is not unusual to hear some delighted screams coming from within the space.

Large Animal Cages

Aside from the bat enclosure on Deck One, the cages on Deck Two feature the largest number of fabricated animals on the Ark. Both familiar and relatively unfamiliar medium-to-large reptiles, mammals, and non-mammalian synapsids are depicted. As with the animals on Deck One, each of the figures were carefully crafted after real animals that lived at or near the time of the Flood.

Ictitherium, the hyena kind.

Ark Encounter researchers accounted for more than just your run-of-the-mill animal varieties. These are rarely-seen reconstructions of creatures like these chalicotheres, odd-toed ungulates like horses, rhinos, and tapirs. Short hindlegs and long forearms gave them a somewhat gorilla-like stance, though they resemble the unrelated giant ground sloths.

Even staples of Noah's Ark animal scenes look a bit different. Featuring a shorter neck and four ossicones, the Ark Encounter giraffes better represent known ancient varieties within the giraffe kind than do modern forms.

Three-dimensional sculpting technology helped ensure anatomical accuracy and allowed the Ark Encounter artists to develop custom poses. Some were partially or fully 3D-printed, like these non-mammalian synapsids modeled after *Cynognathus.*

A handful of dinosaur figures can be seen on the Ark, like the stegosaurs above. However, not every dinosaur-looking sculpture represents a dinosaur. The figures to the right, for instance, depict non-dinosaurian reptiles called silesaurs.

Located along the midline light-well of Deck Two, these enclosures allow for up-close viewing of the animals from multiple angles. This exhibit is both experiential and educational, offering life-sized animal figures in staged cages and signs with fun facts about the displayed kinds. In addition to the "fun facts" signs, there is information relating to the biblical "unicorn," managing potential carnivores on the Ark, and more.

Examples of displayed animals include a pair of entelodonts (extinct mammals that look something like a cross between a wolf and a pig); small, low-horned rhinoceroses; pug-nosed crocodile-like simosuchuses; lanky hyenas; juvenile tyrannosaurs; antelope-like cattle; saber-toothed marsupials; and long-faced, otter-like pakicetids—a supposed evolutionary ancestor of whales.

Overall, this exhibit provides an interesting and unconventional look at the sorts of animals Noah and his family maintained on the Ark. These animal figures only scratch the surface of the true imaginativeness of our Creator, while the enclosures provide a glimpse at the potential ingenuity of our ancestors on the Ark.

Animal Care Working Scenes

T he themed Deck Two animal enclosures display full-scale representations of potential designs for time-saving animal care systems. Included are semi-automated food and water feeders. Members of Noah's family can be seen utilizing the overhead catwalks or even feeding a favorite animal by hand.

These large animal enclosures include feeding systems that consist of funneled bamboo chutes leading from the catwalks to food troughs in the cages below. The watering systems offer a similar degree of automation. Massive, vacuum-fed water tanks maintain water levels in dishes accessible from two or more enclosures. When the tanks are drained, they can be refilled from the catwalk by prying a central rod upward, which simultaneously corks the lower outlet and uncorks the upper inlet. The reverse process restores the vacuum seal.

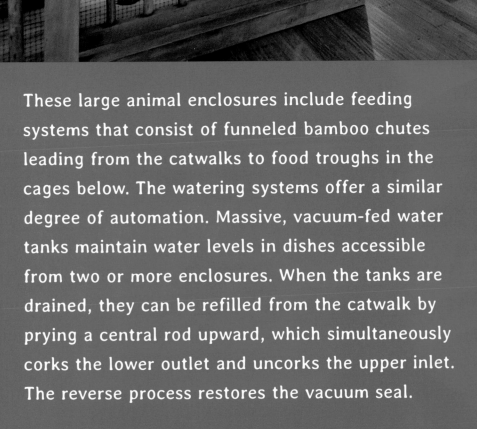

Animal Kinds Exhibit

A common question voiced by believers and skeptics alike is, "How could Noah fit all the animals on the Ark?" The key to understanding this issue is that Noah and his family brought only *land-dependent* animals with them on the Ark, and of those, they brought representatives from every kind. Since kinds are typically made up of numerous different species, this means that God only brought select land-dependent representatives of each kind to the Ark.

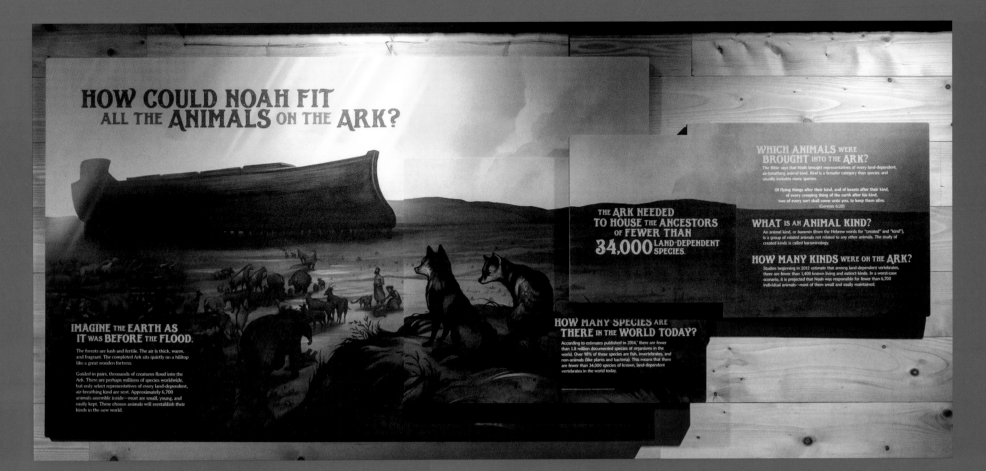

The Animal Kinds teaching bays discuss topics like how many species there are in the world today, what a "created kind" is, the potential mechanisms for the generation of new species within kinds, the differences between biblical creationism and forms of evolution, and the significant shortcomings of the latter. Displayed animal figures include representatives of the dog, cat, *Archaeopteryx,* and great ape kinds.

Animal Care

This extremely popular exhibit explores questions that most people have never considered. How could the small cages be designed to minimize precious time for feeding and cleaning up after the animals? How were small reptiles and amphibians housed and fed? How did Noah's family provide for animals with picky diets, such as koalas and anteaters?

The second bay of this exhibit focuses on some large-scale issues concerning the Ark. How could Noah's family collect enough water for drinking and cleaning? How was the Ark ventilated and lit? How could they efficiently remove waste?

Dioramas and interactive videos demonstrate possible techniques used on the Ark to automate some of the daily chores involved in caring for a large number of animals.

Noah's Study

Noah and his wife can be found in the study. Emzara is seen reading a letter while the lifelike animatronic Noah is ready to answer more than a dozen questions. You can learn about his favorite and least favorite animals and his thoughts about the world before the Flood. You might even hear him flirt a little with his wife.

Library

The Ark's library features plenty of scrolls and clay tablets to counter the popular notion that people in ancient times were incapable of reading and writing. To give guests some insight into Noah's personality, as imagined by the Ark Encounter, the exhibit includes several personal items Noah and his wife collected over the years.

Workshop

The fact that Noah built the Ark demonstrates his proficiency in woodworking, so it should come as no surprise to see a workshop in the Ark. This room serves as another reminder that, contrary to popular opinion, ancient people were intelligent and highly skilled.

Being on the Ark for about a year with thousands of animals would inevitably require maintenance. Damaged cages and tools could be repaired or replaced. It is also possible that someone on board the Ark worked with wood as a hobby.

Blacksmith

Genesis 4:22 describes Tubal-Cain as an instructor of bronze and iron craftsmen. It is possible that one or more of Noah's family members learned this trade as well, which could come in handy during the year of the Flood.

The light well in the middle of the Ark allows light from above to spill to the lower levels and offers some amazing views of the Ark's spectacular timbers and craftsmanship.

Who Was Noah?

The Bible gives us a few details about Noah. He was a righteous and faithful man. Using artistic license while staying within biblical parameters, the Ark Encounter team developed a backstory for Noah to explain how he may have acquired the skills necessary to build the Ark.

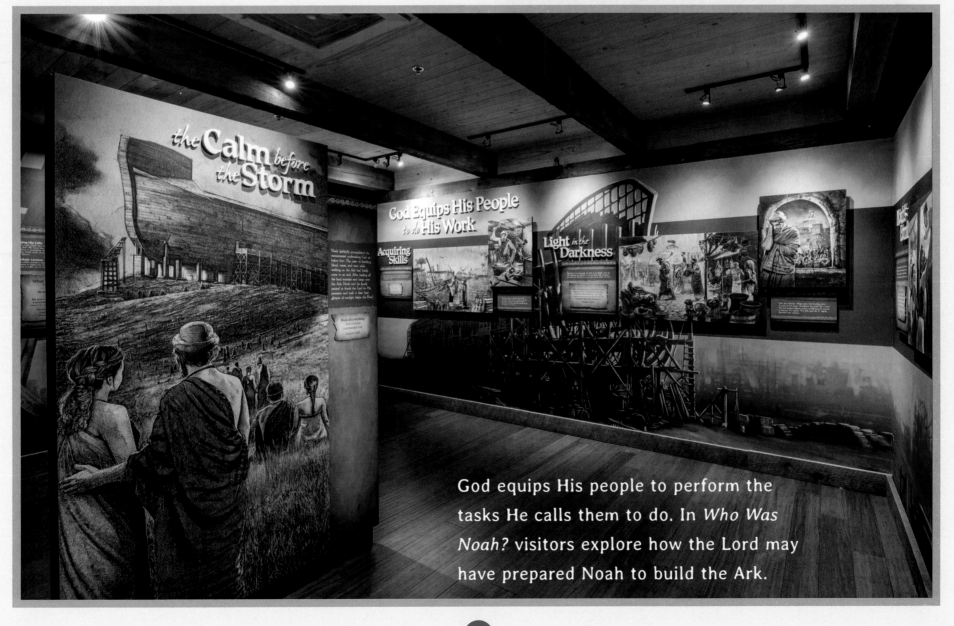

God equips His people to perform the tasks He calls them to do. In *Who Was Noah?* visitors explore how the Lord may have prepared Noah to build the Ark.

Fairy Tale Ark

Cute, whimsical, adorable. Those words accurately describe most depictions of Noah's Ark, giving the dangerous impression that the biblical account was simply a fairy tale. But the Genesis account highlights God's judgment on an extremely wicked world and His amazing grace shown to Noah's family and the animals aboard the Ark, and it serves as a reminder of the coming judgment.

What would actually happen to one of these fairy tale arks during the Flood? This satirical poem answers that question by concluding, "No man or beast lived happily ever after."

The Door

Imagine being one of eight people in the entire world to survive a catastrophe. What questions would you have? Near the Ark's door, Japheth's wife struggles with difficult questions related to how a loving God could allow so much death and suffering.

The door is one of the most popular places to photograph in the Ark. It reminds us that there was one door into the Ark for Noah's family to enter to be spared from the Flood. Similarly, there is only one way by which a person can be spared from eternal judgment: the gospel of Jesus Christ.

Live Animal Area

Animals from Ararat Ridge are taken to this area of the Ark for guests to experience. Zookeepers teach visitors some amazing details about the incredible creatures that our infinitely wise Creator put on the earth for us to enjoy.

Shem's Room

The Ark Encounter team divided Noah's attributes up among his sons. Like his father, Shem has a deep love for the Lord and is shown reading a scroll during some of his downtime. Each bedroom in the Living Quarters highlights the interests of the couple that lives in it.

Japeth's Room

Genesis 4:21 mentions musical instruments prior to the Flood. Japeth is shown playing a flute, while his wife Rayneh displays her artistic talent and livens the place up a little by painting some pottery.

THE LOOM

Garden Area

The Living Quarters includes many items Noah's family would use for everyday life on the Ark. The loom pictured above could have been used for making clothing, rugs, or other items for the family.

A large garden area is also featured near the light well in this area. Herbs and vegetables that thrive in low-light conditions could have supplemented family meals. The third deck would receive more sunlight than the others if the Ark had the capability to let light in from the roof area.

Kitchen

While most of the foodstuffs would be stored elsewhere in the Ark, the kitchen in the Living Quarters area is stocked with a variety of herbs and spices, as well as a range of utensils for preparing meals for the family. Shem's wife, Ar'yel, can be seen working on a dish.

A stone oven would be used for baking bread and a selection of cooking vessels for making soup or hot drinks.

Dining

The dining area has space for all eight family members to enjoy a meal or to discuss important matters and pray together.

Ham and his wife, Kezia, enjoy each other's company as they prepare some vegetables for the family meal.

Ham's Room

This room provides a perfect place for Ham and Kezia to relax after a long day of work. It reveals many of their interests, such as Ham's engineering prowess and Kezia's skill in treating injuries and illnesses.

Noah's Room

In addition to being a place for Noah and Emzara to sleep, this area showcases many of their hobbies. Some of Noah's maps and writings are on display, and Emzara's animal sketches can also be seen.

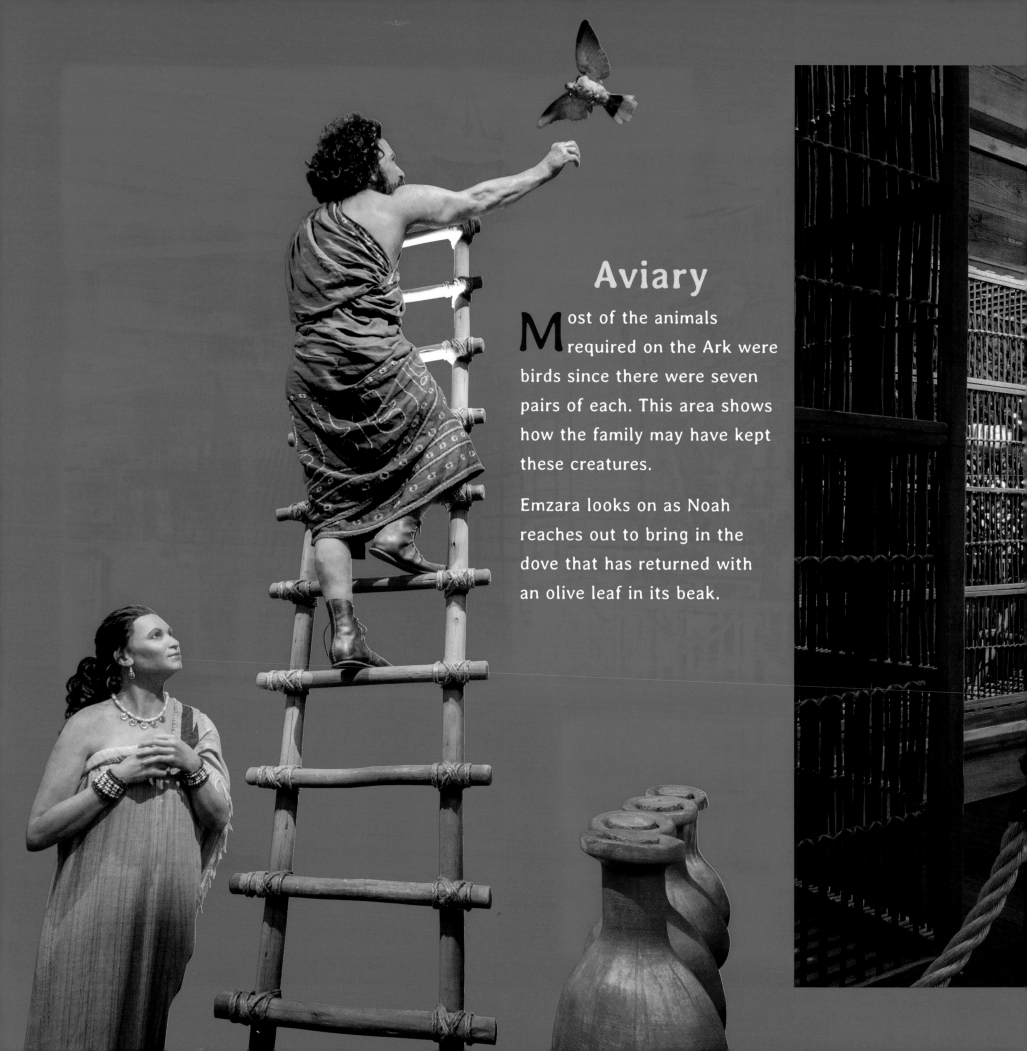

Aviary

Most of the animals required on the Ark were birds since there were seven pairs of each. This area shows how the family may have kept these creatures.

Emzara looks on as Noah reaches out to bring in the dove that has returned with an olive leaf in its beak.

Deck Three Theater

The second and third decks of the Ark's stern end contain theaters, giving guests an opportunity to rest.

The film on Deck Two is about Noah doing an interview with a tabloid reporter. As she mocks him, Noah explains the purpose of the Ark and warns her of the coming judgment. The film on Deck Three brings back the same actors for an updated interview about why the Ark Encounter was built and features a powerful gospel presentation.

Architecture in the Ark

There is no shortage of amazing views within this spectacular structure. Even the large ramp pictured below is a sight to behold and provides unique glimpses of the magnificent craftsmanship throughout the Ark.

Is this what gopherwood looks like? No one knows for certain since the word only appears in Genesis 6:14, and we are unsure if any modern trees are derived from it. The Ark Encounter includes a variety of wood. The "lodge poles" are Englemann spruce, the massive squared timbers throughout are Douglas fir, the exterior is radiata pine, and the flooring is made of bamboo.

Flood Geology

One of the most important issues related to the Flood account is the science of geology. In fact, it was in this area that secularists first promoted millions of years in an effort to undermine Scripture decades before Darwin published his work.

The Flood Geology exhibit makes this fairly complex subject easy to understand. Beginning with an explanation that creationists and evolutionists study the same facts, the exhibit describes the worldviews through which the data is interpreted.

The exhibit calls attention to multiple areas of geologic study and asks which view makes more sense of what we observe: rapid formation as a consequence of the Flood or gradual formation over millions of years. In each case, the Flood makes better sense of the data.

This area perfectly illustrates the bias against the biblical Flood account. Based on evidence found on Mars, many scientists believe the planet endured massive catastrophic flooding. But many of these same scientists reject a Flood on earth, even though it has an abundance of the same type of evidence and approximately 70% of its surface is covered with water.

Ice Age

Biblical creationists believe there was a single ice age that was triggered by the Flood. The popular secular view posits multiple ice ages, each lasting tens of thousands of years. Which view fits the data better?

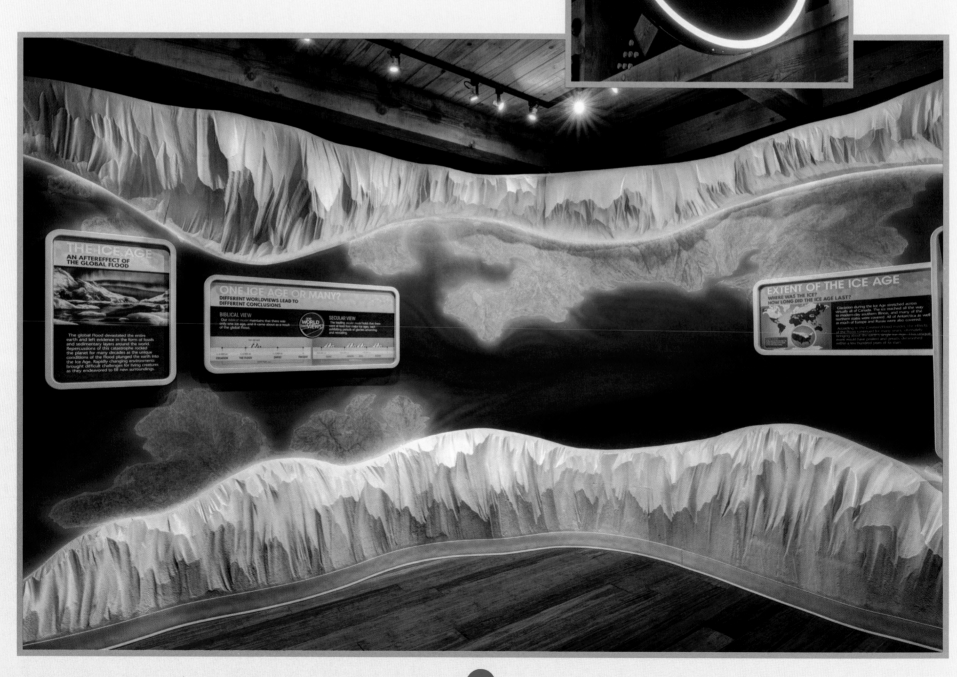

GIANTS OF THE ICE AGE

This cool exhibit highlights evidence for the Ice Age, explains why some of the animals grew so large at the time, and shows how the Ice Age assisted the migration of people and animals around the globe after the Flood.

Secular models explaining how an ice age could start must fudge temperatures by as much as 50 degrees Fahrenheit. The exhibit shows how the unique conditions caused by the Flood give the only known mechanism for generating an ice age: significantly increased ocean temperatures and greatly decreased air temperatures over land.

A detailed diorama and video also illustrate that the massive ice sheets full of so-called "annual layers" do not take long ages to form.

BABEL

The Babel event in Genesis 11 gives us the proper foundation for understanding so much of what we observe in our world today.

The biblical account explains the origin of our language families, but it also helps us understand the variations in people groups and that there is no biblical justification for racism.

After the Flood, God instructed man to be fruitful and multiply and fill the earth. Yet within a few generations, humans rebelled against their Creator again. They gathered together in the plain of Shinar and decided to make a name for themselves by building a city and a tower whose top reached the heavens. God judged these people for their rebellion by confusing their languages. No longer able to effectively communicate, the people dispersed and filled the world.

The remarkable diorama pictured below includes nearly 1,000 individually painted, 3D-printed people building the tower along with around 300 animals.

Reminders of this event might be seen in ancient architecture around the globe. Large ziggurats, pyramids, and ceremonial mounds are found throughout the Americas, Africa, Europe, and Asia. Many of these structures share similar designs and seem to have been built for similar purposes. Are these towers evidence of the biblical event?

Our world is permeated by false views about our early ancestors. Evolutionists portray early man as unintelligent, ape-like brutes. Many Christians have even adopted unbiblical ideas on this subject as they mistakenly think of early man as primitive because they did not possess our modern technologies.

The Ancient Man exhibit clears up these misconceptions by showing evidence that early man was far more intelligent than many people assume. It also corrects many of the false assumptions about our ancestors and what they allegedly believed. What we find in the world matches what Scripture teaches—humans have been intelligent from the beginning, having been made in God's image.

Which view of ancient man does a better job of explaining the evidence: the biblical model or the evolutionary model? The Ancient Man exhibit builds a compelling case that what we observe matches God's Word and contradicts the evolutionary worldview.

Flood Legends

There are over 200 legends about a massive, global flood found in cultures around the world. While they differ from the biblical account in some ways, there are often enough similarities to make the case that many of these tales are distorted retellings of the same event. But the Bible provides the true historical account. The biblical Ark is also the only vessel which could have survived the worldwide Flood and kept its passengers safe.

Rainbow Covenant

Many of the details from Genesis 7–9 are depicted in this stunning piece in the Rainbow Covenant exhibit. After the Flood, Noah offered a sacrifice to God of the clean animals and flying creatures. God blessed Noah and his sons and instructed them to be fruitful and multiply. He said that the rainbow would be the sign of His promise to never again flood the earth with water.

The Voyage of a Book

The Bible is by far the best-selling book in history. In this artifact-filled exhibit, visitors will experience several snapshots of how the Bible spread around the world to become the most-translated book of all time.

Featuring numerous ancient manuscripts, the exhibit takes visitors on a journey from the place where much of the Bible was written, Israel, to various locations around the globe. Beginning with biblical characters like Ezra and Paul, the exhibit highlights certain individuals who brought God's Word to a new region. Discover the impact made by Frumentius in Ethiopia, Myles Coverdale in England, Hudson Taylor in China, Carl Strehlow in Australia, and many others who propagated Scripture in unreached areas.

The exhibit also asks visitors to consider the role they will play in taking God's message even farther.

SAUL / PAUL

It is the job of a Pharisee to make sure **everyone follows the Law.**

These followers of Jesus, people of the Way, are **reinterpreting the Law,** claiming he is the Messiah.

Saul **won't let that happen.**

Suddenly, with a flash of light, **everything is different.**

Saul **encounters Jesus.**

Unable to contain himself, Saul travels to cities and towns all over Israel telling people what happened to him on the road to Damascus, **urging them to believe in Jesus of Nazareth as the prophesied Messiah.**

But he is rejected over and over again.

His people don't understand this change of heart, just as he didn't understand before that day on the road.

So Saul leaves Israel.

He **begins his new journey with a new purpose** and a new name.

Saul, **now Paul,** sets sail to Syria, Greece, and Rome.

Along the way, he writes letters of instruction and encouragement to the new churches in these areas. These letters **become a major part** of the Christian New Testament.

"But Saul was ravaging the church, and entering house after house, he dragged off men and women and committed them to prison." (Acts 8:3, ESV)

"And he said to me, 'Go, for I will send you far away to the Gentiles." (Acts 22:21, ESV)

**Karaite Prayer Book,
Kedushah Prayer Section**
These pages were recovered from the Cairo Genizah (a sacred storehouse) in a synagogue in Egypt.
In Hebrew
Paper
Cairo (Egypt)
1300s

**Karaite Prayer Book,
Evening Prayers**
These fragments show the presence of a vibrant Jewish community in Egypt.
In Hebrew
Paper
Cairo (E...

HUDSON TAYLOR

A young British man decides to leave home.

So he boards a ship bound for Shanghai.

Wanting to fit in, Hudson starts dressing like the locals and wearing his hair in Chinese fashion.

Because of this he is ridiculed and questioned by his friends and colleagues.

They don't understand.

The Chinese, however, accept him. They listen when he tells them about the Bible.

And even though he is still learning the language, he sets off to distribute Bibles and tracts in Chinese.

That is, until he gets sick.

So sick in fact that he has to return to England.

Hudson is so discouraged and sad that he has to leave his beloved China.

But he decides to make good use of his time. He begins translating the Bible into Mandarin.

Eventually, Hudson returns.

He establishes the China Inland Mission.

The Bible continues to spread across China today.

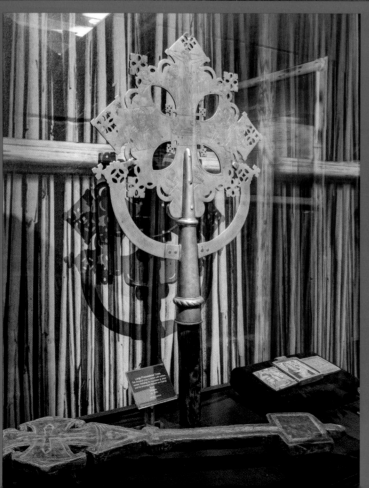

The Voyage of a Book exhibit is unique in the Ark Encounter in that it is the only exhibit developed by an outside organization. As they have done at the Creation Museum, representatives of the Museum of the Bible have put together a spectacular exhibit featuring manuscripts and other artifacts from their extraordinary collection.

The Why the Bible Is True exhibit invites guests to follow Gabriela, Ryo, and Andre around their college campus as they seek to find answers to some of life's most important questions.

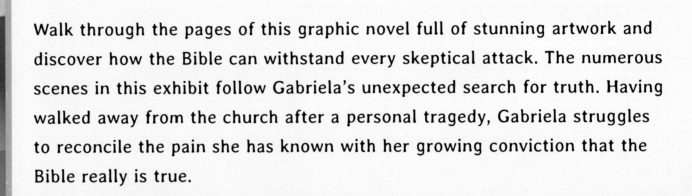

Walk through the pages of this graphic novel full of stunning artwork and discover how the Bible can withstand every skeptical attack. The numerous scenes in this exhibit follow Gabriela's unexpected search for truth. Having walked away from the church after a personal tragedy, Gabriela struggles to reconcile the pain she has known with her growing conviction that the Bible really is true.

Then the LORD said to Noah, "Enter the Ark, you and your whole family, for I have found you righteous before Me in this generation."

— GENESIS 7:1 —

The blood shall be a sig
where you live. And when
over you, and the plac
to destroy you when I s

— EXODU

THE BIBLE TELLS US THAT MEN HAD BECOME EXCEEDINGLY WICKED—THEY THOUGHT OF EVIL CONTINUALLY—SO GOD PLANNED TO FLOOD THE EARTH AND WIPE THEM OUT.

HE TOLD NOAH TO BUILD AN ARK AND TO PUT A DOOR IN ITS SIDE. WHEN GOD SHUT THE ARK'S DOOR IT PICTURED HIS JUSTICE AND HIS MERCY.

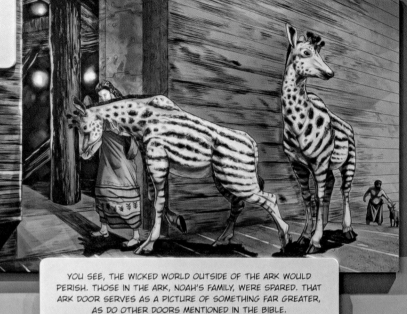

YOU SEE, THE WICKED WORLD OUTSIDE OF THE ARK WOULD PERISH. THOSE IN THE ARK, NOAH'S FAMILY, WERE SPARED. THAT ARK DOOR SERVES AS A PICTURE OF SOMETHING FAR GREATER, AS DO OTHER DOORS MENTIONED IN THE BIBLE.

ABOUT A THOUSAND YEARS AFTER THE FLOOD, GOD USED MOSES TO LEAD THE ISRAELITES OUT OF SLAVERY IN EGYPT.

THE NIGHT BEFORE THEY WERE SET FREE, THE LORD INSTITUTED THE PASSOVER. ISRAELITES WERE TOLD TO SACRIFICE A LAMB WITHOUT BLEMISH, AND THEN PUT SOME OF THE LAMB'S BLOOD ON THE FRAMES AROUND THEIR DOORS.

ou on the houses
ne blood, I will pass
not fall on you
e land of Egypt.

It is impossible for the blood of bulls
and goats to take away sins.
— HEBREWS 10:4 —

NEARLY 500 YEARS AFTER MOSES, KING SOLOMON BUILT THE FIRST TEMPLE IN JERUSALEM. TWO DOORS WERE PLACED AT THE ENTRANCE TO THE INNER SANCTUARY, THE PLACE OF GOD'S HOLY PRESENCE.

THOSE WHO FAITHFULLY FOLLOWED THE LORD'S INSTRUCTIONS WERE SPARED FROM THE TENTH PLAGUE—THE DESTRUCTION OF THE FIRSTBORN. THEY WERE PROTECTED FROM GOD'S JUDGMENT BY THE BLOOD OF A LAMB.

BECAUSE SIN SEPARATES US FROM GOD, ONLY THE CEREMONIALLY CLEAN HIGH PRIEST COULD ENTER THESE DOORS ONCE A YEAR TO OFFER SACRIFICE FOR THE SINS OF THE PEOPLE.

Near the end of this exhibit, visitors will encounter a unique presentation of the gospel called the Doors of the Bible. This series of doors highlights biblical history while explaining important background information about the gospel.

Learn how the Ark's door, the blood around the Israelites' doors at Passover, the doors to the holy of holies in the temple, and the door of the sheepfold point forward to Christ's sacrificial death for our sins on the Cross. Three days later, Jesus conquered death and walked out of the door of the empty tomb.

Guests will see how Gabriela and Ryo respond to the gospel. Will they choose the broad gate that leads to destruction or walk through the narrow gate that leads to life?

HANDMADE & FAIR TRADE

Gift Shop

Awide variety of resources and souvenirs can be found in the Ark's gift shop. A large fair trade section of the store allows guests to support people in poverty-stricken regions by purchasing unique items made by individuals in those places.

Emzara's Kitchen

Be sure to bring your appetite. The Ark's expansive restaurant features plenty of delicious items in its large buffet.

Dozens of spectacular mounts and dynamic paintings of animals from all over the world can be viewed throughout the large dining room.

Zip Lines

The zip lines and challenge courses at the Ark Encounter give visitors some unique vantage points as they look out at this beautiful piece of land.

More difficult than it appears at first glance, the Eagle's Nest Aerial Adventure course offers options for adults and children to test their abilities in the air.

Get ready to fly! The Screaming Eagle zip lines feature two dozen lines that will provide plenty of thrills for the adventurous at heart. By using the state-of-the-art harness system and following the safety policies, visitors can relax and enjoy the ride.

Ten of the super-zip lines are about 1,000 feet long and two of these are nearly twice that long. On some lines, guests will approach speeds of nearly 50 miles per hour and soar more than 170 feet above the ground.

Soar above the canopy and take in some amazing views of the Ark.

Ararat Ridge Zoo

Located on the northwest side of the Ark is Ararat Ridge, an outdoor attraction featuring a small zoo, petting zoo, and animal rides. While the artistic depictions inside the Ark represent some of the creatures Noah and his family maintained on the Ark, the zoo features live examples of certain kinds that survived the Flood. There, guests will encounter exotic animals like alpacas, emus, kangaroos, llamas, ostriches, yaks, and zebras. Signs and on-site personnel are present, providing information and assistance.

The paved trails around the zoo allow guests to get close to the animals, like the red kangaroo pictured to the left. New animals will be featured at the zoo so that guests can learn more about God's amazing creatures.

Petting Zoo & Animal Rides

Unlike an increasing number of zoos, Ararat Ridge offers a more interactive experience than just viewing animals from outside their enclosures.

Access to the petting area is included with the Ark's general admission, allowing for direct contact with some of the fluffy residents of Ararat Ridge.

For the adventurous guest who desires even greater excitement than petting the animals, donkey and camel rides are made available daily during the warmer months (conditions permitting). Ararat Ridge is truly a place that the whole family can enjoy!

Outside the Ark Encounter

Magnificent rainbows have been photographed near the Ark, a beautiful reminder of God's promise to never again destroy the world with a flood.

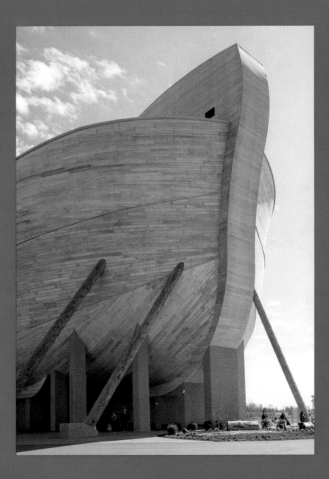

At 300 cubits in length (510 feet based on a 20.4 inch cubit), the Ark is "bigger than imagination." A wonder to behold, the Ark is a reminder of God's tremendous mercy and grace in the midst of His righteous judgment on sin.

THINK
BIGGER